Celebrations in the Ossuary

Kyle J. Knapp

Copyright © 2013 by Meta L. Knapp

All Rights Reserved. No part of this book may be reproduced in any form or by any means without the prior written consent of the publisher, except where permitted by law.

Cover images from iStock (www.istockphoto.com); Design by dMix.
Artwork by Kyle J. Knapp.
Author photograph by Eustina Daniluk.

ISBN: 978-0-9833775-7-3

BEAT to a PULP
PO Box 173
Freeville, New York 13068

Email: btapzine@beattoapulp.com
Visit us at www.beattoapulp.com

Contents

Introduction	i
The Paper Towel Heart	1
To Drink in Early Hours	2
Camping	4
We Lived Alone	6
Edward and Dedalus	8
The Warren	10
The Perfect Day	11
Four Summers Ago	12
The Greatest Loss	14
Writing Letters Alone in the Light of the Alcove	18
The Lake House Lights	20
Grimm Dreaming Rancor	22
The Hotel Piano	23
How Selfish Were Her Eyes?	24
Anna	26
The Voice	28
A Hairless Satan at the Oriel	29
Another Time	30
The Whole of the World Is Rotting	31
We Fell Below the Earth	34
Her Ghost in the Courtyard	38
The Searchlights	40
The Glass Room of Orcus and Selene	42
Sad Flower Fences in Hordes Aglow	44
Howell, the Hero	46
The Last Sun	47
The Pastoral Pastor, Pronounced	48
When Will to the Bottle's Rise	50
The Haunt	52
Celebrations in the Ossuary	54
Afterword	57

Introduction

Near the beginning of T. S. Eliot's *The Waste Land* the speaker says, "I will show you fear in a handful of dust." And quite a fear it is, appearing in the opening section "The Burial of the Dead," and evoking the biblical reminder of our ultimate return to the earth. A similar reminder appears in the title of this work, *Celebrations in the Ossuary*. An ossuary is a place for bones of the dead, oftentimes many dead. But where Eliot gives us fear, Kyle Knapp offers a celebration. In the ossuary! And what sort of celebration might we expect in a storage container for bones? Paradoxically, it is a celebration of life.

In "Camping" we see the joy of nights in the woods, so pleasant that for the rest of the year "nothing at all seemed to matter." Or it is a perfect day composed of simple pleasures and ending with "her laughter." Even when "Writing Letters Alone in the Light of the Alcove" it is a celebration of "… three men / Drunk and dancing on the ocean floor."

But it is an ossuary, and these poems capture the loss, the regret, the acknowledgement of ultimate doom. There is an edge to the celebration, the clear sense that much of what brings pleasure brings pain as well. While Eliot gives us fear, Kyle Knapp reminds us that life is worth celebrating, even though "Every bone / dust."

Philip Tate
Professor of English
Tompkins Cortland Community College
August, 2013

The Paper Towel Heart

I wish that I could be a legitimate bard
A scarred up, sacred emblem
For the paper towel company
With a fishing lure draped from red rotten flannel
That exposes, through rusty louvered threads
A story book tattoo that claims a woman as his

But I can't live up to that shit! No fucking way
I've got the soggy heart of a poet
The maudlin ill-at-ease of a drunk
I cry when I look out the window
And I still can't see past the stars.

Born into Trouble as the Sparks Fly Upward
Is one of the greatest, and most depressing albums ever composed
And why the hell I put it on, as the car lights left that same window
And my family went away
I'll never claim I could ever know

To Drink in Early Hours

The first drink is never eudemonism wronged by sorrow
It is never a wrong to the expense or expanse of the hearts
    contracted condition,
Or to cherished friends, or to a lovers lost love
The first drink is always nostalgia, and never to *drink* itself
Never to itself—the grand joy of sickness
Because *that* is always wanton,
irreproachable
and condemned to nowhere:

The first drink is the ego remembering its long-lost greatness
A recapitulation to the loss of our very greatest need as men and
    mankind
For the control of our own lives forevermore
Fostering, with the swallow a sound and inescapable denial—
Of the greater, inescapable need
To escape

(an artificial need ... and more compelling ... than anything
    human)

It is a revolt against the immutable script;
Of The Sentence of Disease
The loss of origin,
The nails pounded through the veins of the locus

And at the time, you really do feel your soul returning
You really do!
You feel the flowers warming to touch,
You feel the mind swell,
Assuming original chords and chorus, Assuming life—
Balance and Grace and Wonder
And you know that *Now* you can command your right
To live like everyone else does
In every bar across Ameri-corp
(In this rotted heathen culture you were born to adore)
But you wake up alone
 Naked again
on the floor,
With a broken ankle in vomit
And you <u>Honestly</u> don't know how the hell you failed
Four thousand times
 And you note that you may never be convinced.

Camping

For fourteen springtime nights we camped
In a row of tents along the ridge
And the darkened amethyst creek bed
Poured liquorish blue below our raucous fires
Until then,
 the mild sunbreak
Or someone who was still awake,
Threw in the first line.

I had hollowed a rise of dead oak
To mortar our tar-black coffee grounds
And I pretended I knew the time
By staring at the sky.

One night it rained hard
And I wrote a poem called "Pluvial Gardens"
With a raging contact high,
Of pink-lightning and wine.

Scared stupid by Hollywood superstitions
I slept near the lantern until day
In the light-saber-blue doom neon
That waited for dangerous flies.

Then there was the poignant bliss of pulling in my first pike
It was like a childhood birthday,
But with whiskey and eggs
In the creamy tangerine twilight
(which nobly enfolded the stream
With the rare escape of the sublime)
Where we paraded with our women
Into the mysteries of the vine.

Silver Patron, with a flavored rose
For falling ill in the stormy marigolds
With her lost in the darkened nowhere
With the lantern shattered in the grass
We walk on each other's feet to find another place to camp

Fireworks colored the close of our halcyon days away
As goodbye's passed under the opalescent banks
And cars lit up, harrowing rust and tanned tires
And for yet another year,
Nothing at all seemed to matter.

WE LIVED ALONE

We lived alone,
We lived alone on the banks of heaven
We lived alone in this cavern hall.
And don't you at all remember?

The apples were hidden in your hand
The blue-gemmed garlands of forever falling sand
Dusted the mirage of the quarry

Don't you remember,
When and where you died?
 Gravity then (some new *curse*)
 Had begun to slow the world
her pale pulse
—So barely had it held through

I was asleep, barely breathing
But I knew you were running along the promenade through time
Through the avalanche of the blue-darkening sand
Where most of us were lost

I heard my name when you cried,
Through dreams, through time
when you fell on the ice
caught your hair in thorns

And I knew,
 you were alone
And I would be alone again forever.

And I couldn't help you stand
I couldn't hold your hand,
When his eyes turned black
And everyone fell dead
Burst into flame.
A thousand-corpse field
Was then carried away across the sky
 —a floating island
A paradise
 turned pale ash
     And lost,
 forever.

Edward and Dedalus

Can I still walk?
Or speak
Can I breathe?
Will my spine estuary?
Does purple blood betray my collar
Of bone's lurid laurel of colors?

Being a drunk is not unlike the lore of lycanthropy,
In a way;
The way the soft silken skin is rent,
The ripened heart whitened
Is not it unlike the dead when dying
 Exposed under the lamp?

You see Mr. Hyde leaping frantically from roof to roof
He leers at you, and falls into the harbor,
Hairy palms claw the surface edge, ebb flowing
—Backwards into the sewers.

There are wormholes in the forest bleeding
A Dedalus—manifold—
A card board abyss ripped at the edges
Whence that Timeless
 Hated—
 Criminal fraud
You love to hate
—To hate yourself become,
And to become soon enough again

Walks forth
The labyrinth
From within

His Cancerous
  Colossus-of-Death
Smile/smirk
Pushes back the waves
As he remerges from The Lake
At the calling hour
With one arm he pushes down the lighthouse tower,
A Catherine wheel fractures the fog
Throwing bricks upon the shale bed
Dragging behind him
your corpse
With the other arm affixed
 Through shallow evergreen waters
Tied at long by a tinsel rope
He twists around one finger, as
He looks back and laughs.

The Warren

    The Warren
      Blue - Spelled
        In incandescence
          Luminous

    We lie awake
      With heavy eyes
        Exuberant
          Impervious

The Perfect Day

Give me just a day
    Of homemade wine,
Spray-painted sunflowers,
19th century prose,
Sordid, puerile jokes,
Dried maple leaves to crush in our palms
A pale too-old sun to dance beyond

And her laughter—

Four Summers Ago

It's my very own countenance that has lost all of its eternal
    beauty,
Not this ancient forest
Or it's immaculate glistening percussion
Of warm living life.

I used to hear a distant crenulation along the base of the dark
    flagstone wall
And think to myself of the soft foot fall
Of a scared young girl
In a softly parted cloth dress,
Torn from the window sash she's crawled from to see me.

Or I'd think of one of my most cherished friends,
Clumsily carrying himself through the brush to get me stoned
    on grass
At the crack of dawn
before school …

Those days will come again,
They were eternal, after all …

Now I think of fugitives burrowed in the toolshed
In the hedges deep below the valley
Chugging gasoline
Spearing squirrel,

With severed shovel handle
Dancing with mannequins
Under painted snakes
hanging from the willow trees all around
The gourd,
Wild dogs drowning in reach of the ridge
In reach of the afterlife.

Four years ago,
Our blanket soaked in sherbet/chrome
And upon the Cancer Sun
Onto the weather we three lay
Confused and twirling happily
stretched out in the fold of the ridge
At the edge of the ancient forests
Dreaming of wisdom and permanence
I fell asleep, and woke up deplored and sullen
Four years ago,
And woke up today
All alone,
Again.

The Greatest Loss

Aiden Roth Granlin
Taught me sudden balance, and glean
He taught me to walk the embers in such endless demure
    sorrow,
Then to turn backward and wink
Then he'd *run* back through it all at you!
Kicking up whirlpools of scintillating sunshine into his smile

He taught me to pray for wind spell, and ruinous rain
To draw up from the windlass a quart of tequila
For share—for every friend.

He knew the true platonic eternity of "Jouissance"
A *True* Laconian godling pretended for a pull at private revel
(The professor pales and falls from the banister abashed, and
    dead at last)
He would remark horrorshow and harlequin
 All at the same—and *in* the same three seconds
As platonic eternity unfolded still
Into a cellophane clown balloon—pop

I will never forget the misgivings of his wise, seldom smile
But when it was real,
You mourned its pass for days after the day's end passed.

That singular way as when he walked into any room;
All eyes fill the qualm of reserve
Squirming sometimes terrified
For those at the end of his latest offense,
But always there was too a mute revelation
And always and most of all,
The joy of his grandeur
And the strength of his life
It beaconed,
Blessed.

I'll never forget him saying for the first time
"It's not rape if you say surprise!"
(I laughed so god-damn hard.)
Or him telling me with the lightest, loftiest heart
 So many times, and time and time again
With no thought to what crime of indiscretion I had allowed
    myself *this time*
"Kyle, you're o.k.
I've got your back, brother."

I'll never forget his hand on my shaky adolescent shoulder
That gigantic—groping—grip that was half foul humor
Like Rimbaud's Blacksmith swinging his hammer against the
    throat of King Louis the Sixteenth;
And half true love
Enough love for everyone in the world all at once.

My dear brother, dead
You fucked all the pretty girls,
And made the worst of us smile.

We bantered dead-end philosophy
And got thrown out of taverns together,
Arm in arm
Never really singing the same song
And never really knowing for better or worse
The why of it all

When I think of you fondly, I still have to
 shelter against that same shaking shoulder
 My tired hazel eyes
But then I know you'd want something much more
Something of greatness
And something eternal,
I know,
As I will write to your memory
With even greater care some day.

Writing Letters Alone in the Light of the Alcove

Reaching the boarded-up end
Of a garish
Unlit hall
There is a small alcove
I've dressed to write
Letters and poems
And sort my problems.

I have a friend who never leaves a small island
On the amber shore (or chore) he has imagined
To give form to his mind

And another who's always drunken,
Inconsolable, or disconsolate
 Without any care for words
Or the cold forbidden waters
Of tired foreign wars.

We laughed away the concept of "hell"
And *right at*—the dead children
 in back of the theater
like a cat without eyes,
Or a car in the river

Liquor incites every night
romantic wars on other planets
Narrated in tricolor maudlin,
Muddled speech

Time Travel,
And Visions,
 Magic in the dampened veld of African myth,
And other graceless,
 But ever-charming vexations
Endless to our cheering phantasmagoric imaginations

Myself, trying to sleep in the alcove tonight
I wonder how one day I will word
My memory of three men
Drunk and dancing on the ocean floor
Peering into outer space, sadly sordid and
When we were young,
So simple.

The Lake House Lights

I walked past a bleary lake house
With blueberry windows wide as walls
The dour umber vase
 Of the glass-luster universe
Shadowed the blue flagstone piazza
And played with moon-gold clouds
Distant
on furry hills

The softly gemmed lighthouse shimmer
Of a refracted car lane refulgence
Performs a play
—a theme for us
 Like pernicious ships
Banked
in the Reeds of Yore

Who lives up there?
      Who never saw the daylight!
Who never saw the swarming street
Whose blood had dried in the attic
A century or more ago

What little girls leapt
From the sash at midnight?
In to the red-veined arms
Of high school limerence?
And where were you,
When all this happened?
At what time were you born exactly?

Grimm Dreaming Rancor

Dreaming at daybreak
With my head on the piano
In wine splashed spittle, groaning
I had a dream that Mr. Grimm,
From the Twisted Metal Tournament
Was sitting alone at a bench in the park;

He was an old man with a monocle,
    Instead of a motorcycle and a handbag collection of souls
And he offered me a palm of almonds
"Sure," I spoke forth
And with me he shared,
Dividing equally his scanty ration.

The Hotel Piano

The hotel piano played "The Ghost Song"
And restless,
Whiskey warmed workmen
Began to pour into the gutted room
In ever-circling semicircles
Cherishing cigarettes
And pulling at each other's heads

The hall filled
And banisters broke
Still whirling, they spat
Eating hair from each other's beards

The ceiling cracked along everywhere at once
Like a dark red snake skin stretched across the vault of the sky
Fat cement blocks broke down like rain,
And drew blood darker red from
The fattened flannelled drooling patrons
As the wide black piano into mahogany flame suddenly burst
But the song still played,
On until morning.

How Selfish Were Her Eyes?

How selfish were her eyes
How eerie and weary
And wide and bright
The girl who drinks bleach,
And never dies,

She hangs herself from the clothes line
And I don't know why …
Hoarse Angels drinking chartreuse from smashed vases
Look on her from the fireplace,
 sparkling purple adamantine
smiling daylight—dreams of crystal figurine
 Glowing in the dawn
While in the corner she cries,

And when she finally falls
Dire to mirth
I run for water,
Forgiveness,
For years of shelter.
Happily then I do tired rise
To obey the shifts
 in her tireless fever

But then, now at last
I can no longer see her
Not ever from the windows of the floors she wanders
Not in March, when the towers lean west and the ghosts shake
    the surface
And the mad are released into Mountains of Olympus.
Never again,
Never.

Anna

    O
   Anna
—collapsed across the balustrade
—argent, and alone
 in the amber orchards,
Of spectral dreamscape autumn
     Like in the tales of Ardis Hall

    Oh, You remind us all of the nocturne
Where the carmine seawall breaks apart
And some riverside siren laughs and runs away
Into the bleak ~!

 I had a dream once,
When you were just a little girl,
Pretending you had superpowers
In which we would climb an old wooden windmill,
Abandoned in a prairie
And watch thunderstorms
Kicking our summer tanned legs in the umber shadows
Of the great Fall.

A low sepia fog wrapped the banisters
And yellow lightning jumped across time
The warm black-and-white rainfall
Became rich lambent green when it crossed
The rich veil of your dark, lilting eyes.
And I only woke up twice,
A decade or more ago
And I never told you,
Because I never remembered to.

The Voice

Who are you to enter this room?
With cautious candle
With frail tapers
That someone just a dint
Crazier
May eat from your hand
Or the whole hand—
Just now!

How have you not
Left this room
Without your purpose?
With a bandaged hand
With a pint of Arak

How can you have never, ever
Addressed a soft angel
Or a "Noble-winged seraph"
Above the high bough?

What have you left!
If not our wisdom
And what have you tried
If not our kindest smile?

A Hairless Satan at the Oriel

"If only this bedroom had a black light,"
Sighed the haunting at the oriel.
"What do you want!" I barked at the shade.
"Your future," he groaned, and motioned me to follow.

I sat up and asked:
"In the future, do I go with you to the future?
   Then I already know. Go away."
He stood for a moment still,
Growing slowly in height.
I lit a Marlboro smooth, and the ghost
Now filling a wall
Now spilling onto the ceiling
Solidified into a hairless satan
And knifed me in the gut.

Coughing a sandy sheet of warm messy blood, I muttered,
"Go fuck yourself," and closed my eyes.
"You ignorant slut," he said,
   And again he sighed.

Another Time

Magic you ask for
AEAEAE!
No,
I'm sorry I can't be
The Shaman Prince
Philosopher-God
Of the graveyard—
Sunset,
Walking off
Into the sky
—For you

No,
 not any more,
That was another me.

The Whole of the World Is Rotting Outside of This Very Tavern

I've come against this bench to write
The cost of a slower cadence
Perhaps as the "about the artist" column
Is a will of confession
And a little lilting, dolorous song
Is aubade to begin the slower auspice of the dance ...

I've been "three sheets" to the wildest midwestern wind,
 For so many irreplaceable summers,
And so has that cold, apetalous girl,
That I wrote to once
When I was only a boy longing
Just a stone sheet away
She is,
As I begin write to her again

 Great screaming Pig Shit!
Somebody slap me into the fan!
I need to remember
What all this is for—

I need so much more time
Or just a smile
And a shay
For my rotted heart
To cross with me

There are so few years to go
Until "I assume my place
In the Great Below"
Or whatever else we'll never know

That reminds me,
That a creepy kid in a terse plaster mansion
Once tore off all his skin
 And died leaning against a pine tree
Gaunt and painted
Before he wrote his first song

Outside, through another door
(He sang!)
The white shadow of a lonely dancer
Is coughing clouds of blooded lung
Into the clouds of blood
That poisoned her lungs

Such will is the madness that remarks
 Upon the strength of my greatest gift,
Will be the final cause of my fatal ruin

And I believe that it was Adam Fischer, who wrote,
"Whisky is alright in its place. Buts its place is in hell"
And I believe that too.
We don't need this bane.
This country is embarrassing enough
Mad men masturbating into circus tents
Oh la Merica
And I'm already too tired
To swim up from the well tonight.

We Fell Below the Earth

Below the ground
I drink and dance
And reconcile to myself
The most common resolution

Eat the berry,
    Drink the husk
And rot below the ground,
And Die
 and Dance

Die, and again
    And then,

Pictures on the walls of cowboy hats
 and driving gloves pinned to the door mat
Dead dirty merchants embracing cattle
Dance *lowly*
For The Fuck of the Cripples
In the private rain

Sometimes I hear them
Below the ground
The surreptitious cautious rhythm
And I make up my own words
By the light of the swinging lantern
I sing
Forbidden is the mirror
    I never see in the hollows
For They never see;
 For They hollowed too soon

Recline here, respite
Drink for yourself, damn you!
Deranged belly fatted dancer
It's far too late for you,

It's far too late;
For Him to have a reckless erection
For the disease to carry
For the topless sullen dancer
To long suddenly for the sparrows to eat her
For the meat to sallow
Gray upon gray,
    Reaping
    Gray

Oh good god, dear god
 That tortured Kashmir cunt!
What will to that?
In the shades of gray
below the boardwalk

A thousand years
Borne below the clay-born
—the estuary
    The council of cruel insane men will one day say:
"That picture of Jesus isn't even Jewish"
But you can't see it anyway

Death dance stumbles again
Ghosts knock over shit
They're blind folded and banished and deaf
As worm
It's the only explanation
For such callous clumsiness

"I will!" cried the devil
And sorrow filled my glassed words
When I asked just for a greatcoat
To throw into the conflation
Of the melting solarium

My sorrowed words filled upon the pier of our ledge
Fall, GOD
My god.
FALL
Again.

Drain the life from the corpse again
And let us to leave,
Let us live
Let us know who we were
And who we are
And who we may become
When the window swings open once again
From blackness to consciousness

Her Ghost in the Courtyard

You watched the last embers
Fall lilting
From long parted, listless
Lingering lips
To the muddy canvas carpet

The floor crackles,
You look turned down
Cursive vair coronets of smoke
Draw in dance across the casement

And you fainted
Heavily
Falling back
Through the open windows
Without your robes

A traveler steps over your naked, nubile body
Ashed in the garden
Without a glance
Elliptical-electric green rain
Dawns your fake lashes
Putting you out,
Without your glamour.

The Searchlights

The Winter Ceremony
Loll of dance
In the cemetery
Whispers are banished
While the giant green winged birds
 circle the northern ocean
Waiting for the smoke to clear
For their call to come again.

The fogs are carmine and gold
 And lifeless and hollow and old,
They stir pictures in the campfire
And frighten the Indian and the animal away

Sometimes within them children are born
Sometimes within them little girls get lost
Dancing into the white rooms,
Into a parent's picture frame
On the other side of town

The Fogs are pale and senile
Furling and falling
Fervent searchlights
Over cast the garden
 When the great birds draw
And where we're reclaimed by the damned

On the surface of the pale snow,
The forgotten child dies alone.

On the surface of the pale snow,
Forgotten the child dies alone.

The Glass Room of Orcus and Selene

I've accrued a curious and accursed predilection,
Of many somber years;
A preference to foray the heather lost
To watch the world over
 From the darkened towers of Selene
A globe of burnished glass halls, floating in time

The shining clouds, and
The hari searchlights of the heaven-painted coliseum
Reflecting her silver, glittering curtain of violently flowering
    tress
How often she sighs, looking below to
The silent crenulation on the surface of the waters
Torn by the enormous, deathless snakes that have never left the
    oceans
And rise to greet the coming of Man.

I've reasoned that I do have a greater trust for the drowsing
    blandishments of the imagination
Than to the horrid contrast of a stark and disparaging reality
While I sit with Orcus on the floating nettle
The throne of death,
Knotted dead black fronds, coiled in thorn
And glowing red with a living inhuman pulse
We circle the whirlpool of the nebula, not speaking to each
    other for years

I remembered my life,
Imagining the landscapes through the colored glass walls
Of the cold and boundless dream;

My thoughts were always influenced so heavily
By the matrix of lofty, lonely ideal
That I subtly forgot the heartless horseflies,
Hornet's nests,
Malaria and poisons
I happen to discount the wild dogs
And falling stone
My fear of the lechery of the blue, decomposing mountains
Pregnant with lore of the tireless inbred rye farmer
And his seven crooked but personally sharpened teeth-hooks

Siting as a man
Centuries ago
On a patched turquoise quilt,
Drinking Sinicuichi and wine from a cracked wooden bowl
I would gaze past the arbors
And forest slopes
And laugh of the noble joys
Of that romantic mythopoeic savage
I was never wise enough to know

Sad Flower Fences in Hordes Aglow

Sad flower fence in hordes aglow
Rumor the valley's once more in shrine?

Silhouettes of faded factories,
Only the elderly know,
By name
No longer shown the lights
of twilight encampment.

Broken alabaster, cotton mattress springs
Left in the lake to afloat mirage
Sinking like the sinews of a taped together corset
Onto sunken railway—tracks sodden, despoiled
Down thrown

Trains leading only to bookwork today
And the oppressive, listless fame
Of an author waiting to be born
At the end of the next century
To tell us all about them.

The tied together stems of the Gold-Flower crawl
Overtop a rust-rotted icebox,
That's seventeen, or several more, years old
Abandoned by foreign lodgers, or a lover's long leave
At the end of the culvert,
To discolor and corrode.

A caduceus of aquatic, snakelike branches
Were woven through the millrace
To camouflage its longstanding forlorn
Twelve years ago,
When the caretakers passed to their own quiet graves
And the toll could not be borne the throne.

The quiet vale no longer shown
Except through the flowers at the edge, horded aglow
On the quiet quay, at the edge of town
 In September,
And in sorrow,
In poverty
In praise
And pause.

Howell, the Hero

Howell, the hero
How many times
Can we just breakdown
To rampages of ruin

I'm so fucking sorry,
That I wasted something
So fucking beautiful

I'm sorry that I watched this world
Just crumble,
 just fall to shit
And I'm sorry;
That I did nothing
And watched from the roof
Like a god damn fucking moron.

The Last Sun

    On the brilliant, brightest walls lit
        The evening in chains
            Of verdigris mist
    Autumn-colored cloudlets dissolved into the gray gloam
                              Below the byre

Dying,
Through all the centuries
The last sun shivers.

The Pastoral Pastor, Pronounced

I have *pronounced*
You dead
Long gone as if dead
I have pronounced
You as if …

Yes,
 it's better to accept
Our death all along, is it not?

But now I dig into the grave
With opened, writhing
 Wild glassy gaze

My hands have turned red,
Shaking and
Sinking
 Into the stinking molten soil

One eye turned over in the wine
Disfigured,
Looks up at it, and up to me
From the opened alluvium-case casket
Under the undying shafts of moonlight.

I am blinded, and fallen back
Too weak to move
But it's *you* again!

Somehow monstrous
and reamed with ancient red horror-picture incandescence

When then the tongue I sought
Rotted from my mouth
And my eyes, how they fell!
To the base of the bower
And I watched from them, another hour
As if from another dimension
I watched
My entire body collapsing upon itself
Ashing into the meadow, the shell
Every bone
Dust

And visions more
enveloped the world
My sight traveled with formless care
Around the whole of the planet
 whence the mortal coil fell

When I dug up the body then
And touched thy breast
With perverse nimble limb
With grandeur and joy
And pronounced dead, myself
At long last

When Will to the Bottle's Rise

    Placenta moss
        Gladiolus
            A kicked-in lumberyard
                cobwebbed cancer skin tan
                    Ablated by the edge of a tin can
                        Drifting seaside, where
                          And when
                            Will the bottles all rise!

The Haunt

I'm at a heaven side bar
I'm with all of my favorite drinks
And all my favorite friends
From the early years
When we were all wearing wreaths
And somber sex-paint masks

An Ararat Brandy
Arak of Lebanon
Zaya rum from New Zealand
The Great Grouse in the unholy icebox
 A bottle of Dewar's—the usual age of consent
And that bottle of 8-year-old Black Velvet that I left under the
    couch

But it's all a thousand years old by now, or more
Just as we—Immortal.
An innocent specter in the window frame, finally.
And it goes down the frosted stomach
Like the Great Goddess of the East
In "Watching me fall"
Fallen under the wreaths

It doesn't make you drunk now,
As it did then
Oh no;
Because now we don't need it to

Oh Arthur, god bless you
In your blue canoe puking
You *did* know the way to wold

O Western heroes of the midnight war
Gallant beatniks beating off at glass mannequins
With wine-dark tears
You *did* understand the immeasurable beauty
Of the lorn and lost
Of all
that is life.

Celebrations in the Ossuary

If I were celebrated *The Local Poet*
I would no longer reply to vague threats
For harrowing a neighbor's cold roses
In the middle of the night.

The denoted author of the colorless rural hamlet
Has never to abrade his four fingers
Crawling through the coppice
Or burn to death by the harsh neon roseate shadows
Of the sheriff's hell-hound ferrule motor,
Or the amber ambulance glow of the midnight alarm

When the celebrated Idol of rude commune
Is found naked in a tree with four banshee's
A rash forgiveness is known to earn us all even more
    insufferable habits than before
And the gray-eyed weeping creatures
Of the townsfolk lower their pitchforks and firearms
In honor of that special subliminal context
That their young will one day learn to adore
And adopt as well

When a certain *degree* of fame begins to pass, at last
And the honors of the banquet
Are cherished by my wretched house

A village once covered in pale orange grass
 And stippled sand and sleeplessness
And guided around itself by old deer tracks and beer bottle caps
Will then announce at once it's new
 and vulgar
and wildly garish, unthinkable glamour

And Then we can build the graveyard walls around the moor!
With parapet and mortar
 And the hidden caves and secret doors

And only then,
 will the *screams* begin!
And they'll begin to drag the lakes …
Only THEN,
Can you release my severed eye!
For the connubial bloodletting
Come forth tomorrow
Dawn.

†

Afterword

BEAT to a PULP books published Kyle Knapp's *Pluvial Gardens* in July 2012. The eclectic, one-of-a-kind collection touched on nature, death, pop culture, and relationships, interwoven with Greek mythology. A bold, new voice quietly entered the scene, painting what one intuitive reviewer noted as an "impressionistic dreamscape."

Soon after *Pluvial*, Kyle began working on *Celebrations in the Ossuary*. He was so prolific—often writing a poem a day—that he had finished it on October 21, 2012, and at his untimely death on June 18, 2013, he had finished enough for a third book and part of a fourth.

Kyle and I had discussed the direction of his poetry following *Pluvial's* release, and my only suggestion for him was to turn inward and address some of the themes of his life. I knew he had conquered drugs and was in an ongoing fight battling alcoholism. However, it wasn't until after his passing that I started to analyze his work and realize to what extraordinary depth he had mined his soul to lay naked such raw-nerve pieces as "To Drink in the Early Hours" and "Edward and Dedalus." He also warmly opens up his world to reverentially speak of friends he had said goodbye to in "The Greatest Loss" and "We Lived Alone," and he continued to touch on the beauty surrounding him with "The Perfect Day."

For *Celebrations*, I made only minor corrections to Kyle's text. Though he always gave me full editorial control, I didn't feel the need because these verses were resplendent. Kyle often sent a revision telling me to discard what came before, and, more often than not, the revision was from a perfectionist raising his own personal bar with some seemingly slight change. Not much has been altered from Kyle's original work, aside from a few spelling and punctuation corrections and the omission of one word after discussing it with his mother. *Celebrations* is very much the book Kyle wanted published right down to the title, number of poems, artwork, and theme.

On a personal note, I miss Kyle dearly and long to banter with him about Charles Bukowski, Hunter S. Thompson, Vladimir Nabokov, or any number of other authors and books we had discovered and shared. The memories of moments spent in his home along Fall Creek discussing our mutual reading passions are what I'll cherish most, and, I will do my best not to be sad when I recall these memories, because, as Kyle says in these very pages, "Those days will come again,
They were eternal, after all …"

David Cranmer
Freeville, New York
July, 2013

About the Author

Kyle J. Knapp (September 1, 1989 – June 18, 2013) was a poet, musician, and short story writer from Freeville, New York. His debut collection of prose, *Pluvial Gardens*, was released in 2012. He studied Social Sciences at Tompkins Cortland Community College and worked for the school as an English tutor. Kyle enjoyed nature, fishing, and playing guitar. He was a prolific artist, who, at the time of his passing, had written enough material for two additional collections of poetry and a near-complete novel.

*I told her of the pluvial gardens
Of the terse white gloam
Of the rotting billows of ashen snow
That blow the silken frost of hemlock so cold
Swathed in a bower of magenta and stone.*

 BEAT to a PULP
PO Box 173
Freeville, New York 13068

Email: btapzine@beattoapulp.com
Visit us at www.beattoapulp.com

www.ingramcontent.com/pod-product-compliance
Lightning Source LLC
Chambersburg PA
CBHW020021050426
42450CB00005B/581